Ultimate Step by Step Guide to Machine Learning Using Python

Predictive modelling concepts explained in simple terms for beginners

Learn how to train an Artificial Intelligence Model in 7 days!

Text copyright © 2020 Daneyal Anis

All rights reserved.

No part of this book may be reproduced, or transmitted in any form or by any means, electronic, mechanical, magnetic, or photographic, including photocopying, recording, or by any information storage or retrieval system or otherwise, without express written permission of the publisher. No warranty liability whatsoever is assumed with respect to the use of the information contained herein. Although every precaution has been taken in the preparation of this book, the publisher and author assume no responsibility for errors or omissions.

    Published by: Daneyal Anis

    Date of Publication: February 2020

    Language: English

This book is dedicated to my parents who gave me the confidence to chase after my dreams and to my wife & kids who make those dreams worth chasing

Table of Contents

1. Introduction 6
2. Getting Started 7
3. Data Types 10
   - 3.1 Booleans 10
   - 3.2 Numbers 11
   - 3.3 Strings 12
4. Data Structures 14
   - 4.1 Tuples 14
   - 4.2 Lists 15
   - 4.3 Dictionaries 16
   - 4.4 Sets 17
   - 4.5 Custom Objects 19
5. Data Traversing 21
   - 5.1 If Then Else Statements 21
   - 5.2 Loops 23
   - 5.3 Functions 25
6. Data Exploration and Analysis 27
   - 6.1 Explore and Clean Data with Pandas 27
   - 6.2 Find Outliers with Numpy and Scipy 32
   - 6.3 Visualize Data with Matplotlib and Seaborn 36
7. Building Predictive Models 40
   - 7.1 Linear Regression Model 42

7.2 Decision Tree Regression Model 44

8. Understanding Machine Learning.................................... 46

   8.1 Supervised Machine Learning Models 46

   8.2 Unsupervised Machine Learning Models................... 50

   8.3 Deep Learning 52

9. How to Problem Solve Using Machine Learning.............. 56

   9.1 Establish Your Use Case 57

   9.2 Get Agreement on Project Drivers: Time, Cost and Scope 57

   9.3 Confirm If Data Is Readily Available 58

   9.4 Confirm Quality of Your Data..................................... 58

   9.5 Confirm Interpretability of Your Data 59

   9.6 Visualize Your Data.. 59

   9.7 Fit the Right Machine Learning Model to Your Use Case 60

   9.8 Train Your Model... 61

   9.9 Test Your Model 61

   9.10 Productionize Your Model.. 61

   9.11 Iterate!... 62

   9.11 Summary Data Science Workflow 63

10. Conclusion 64

Post your Review 65

Website and Free Gift!.. 66

References 67

1. Introduction

Python was developed in 1980s by Guido Van Rossum of Netherlands. Python was developed as an object-oriented language with an emphasis on simplicity, extensibility and flexibility [1]. Python also comes with a large library of pre-built functionality for data science, statistical analysis and data visualizations which make this language very easy to learn and use.

In this book we will focus on data science applications of Python with hands on examples that allow you to go from novice to expert in a short period of time! We will start with getting you set up with Python, introducing you to its data structures and libraries and then finally getting into the data science applications of this beautiful language.

What you will find different about this book is the visual and hands on approach it takes to teaching Python. Since this book is directed at beginners, we will not drone on and on about complex concepts or make this book text heavy. Instead, we will take inspiration from the Zen of Python by Tim Peters [2]:

"Beautiful is better than ugly…simple is better than complex….sparse is better than dense….".

2. Getting Started

There are detailed instructions available via the Python website on how to install Python on your machine — whether it is Windows, Mac OS or Linux under on Python website in the Getting Started section [3].

I recommend you read through it as there is a lot of good information and helpful links for beginners. However, installing Python by itself is not very helpful or user friendly. You are better off installing Python alongside an IDE (Integrated Development Environment) — as that comes with tools and development environment to execute and debug your code.

For that I recommend starting with Anaconda Distribution [4]. It is an open-source tool that installs industry standard IDEs and foundational Python libraries that we will be describing in this book in more detail. When you click on the above link, it will take you to a page to download and install package for your operating system e.g. Windows, macOS or Linux.

We will be using Jupyter Notebook [5] as our development environment for this book — Jupyter is part of the Anaconda distribution package and will be installed on your machine along with Python.

Jupyter is a powerful web-based development environment that we will be using in this book to execute our code and I have made all the source code used in this book available on my website as a '.ipnyb' Jupyter file. You can access all the code by going to my website here: https://www.daneyalauthor.com and open the code in Jupyter Notebook.

Once Anaconda is installed on your machine, launch Anaconda Navigator from your menu. Screenshot below for reference:

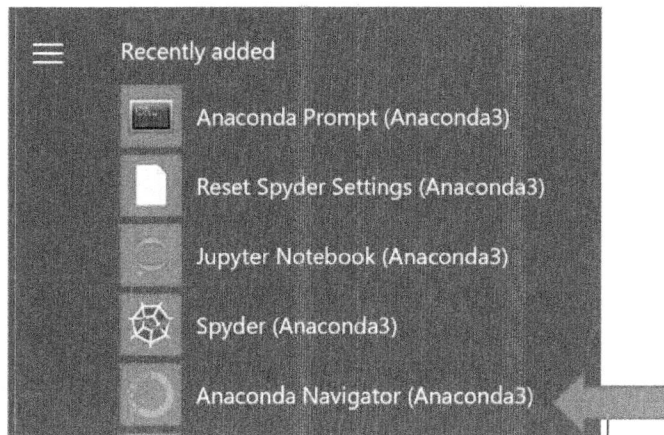

Once open, you should see the following Anaconda Navigator dashboard with all the tools available to you:

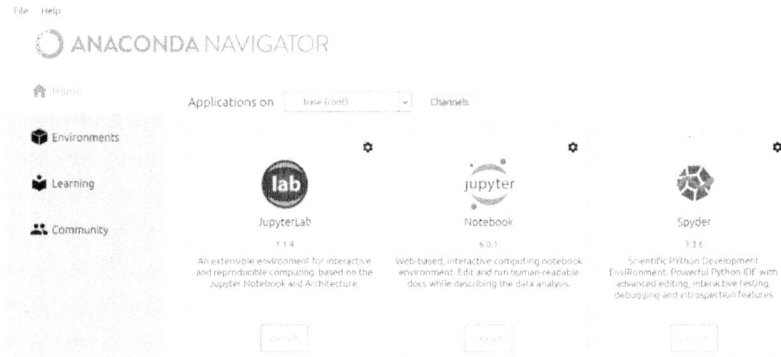

Launch Jupyter Notebook by clicking on the 'Launch' button under that application icon. Once you do that, the following web browser window will open:

Click on 'New' and the 'Python 3' in the top right. Once you do that, a new browser window will open with your new project and Python environment ready to execute. You can rename your project as 'My First Python Project' by clicking on 'Untitled' at the top of the screen (highlighted below for reference).

Done? Alright, you are ready to go!

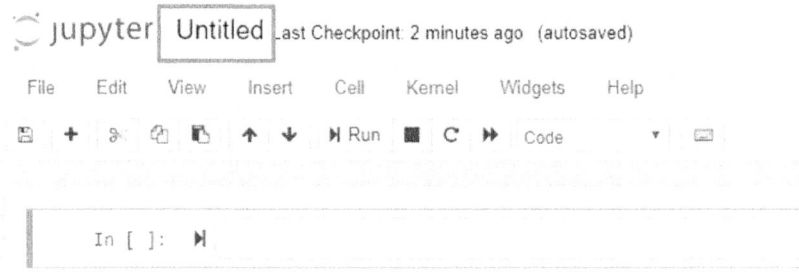

3. Data Types

In Python, there are 3 main types of data types, like most programming languages:

1) Booleans
2) Numbers
3) Strings

3.1 Booleans

Boolean values are True or False. You can use the following Boolean operators to compare different values:

1) Is equal to: ==
2) Is greater than: >
3) Is less than: <
4) Is greater than or equal to: >=
5) Is less than or equal to: <=

Try out this code in the Python notebook you created above as follows:

```
In [1]: 'dan'=='dan'
Out[1]: True

In [2]: 1 >= 2
Out[2]: False

In [3]: 3 == 3
Out[3]: True
```

3.2 Numbers

In Python, numbers can be integers i.e. whole numbers like 1, 2, 3 or floats i.e. numbers with decimals like 1.1, 2.3, 4.5 etc. You can use the basic mathematical operators like:

1) Plus: +
2) Minus: -
3) Multiplication: *
4) Division: /
5) Parenthesis: () to enforce precedence in operations

Try out this code in the Python notebook you created above as follows:

```
In [1]: 1+1
Out[1]: 2

In [2]: 3-2
Out[2]: 1

In [3]: 10/2
Out[3]: 5.0

In [4]: 3*3
Out[4]: 9

In [5]: (5+3)*2
Out[5]: 16
```

You can also check the type of a number by using the type command in Python. See below:

```
In [6]: type(3.5)
Out[6]: float

In [7]: type(12)
Out[7]: int
```

3.3 Strings

Strings are essentially a string of characters. For example, words or sentences. In Python, Strings are designated by single (' ') or double quotes (""). Just like Booleans and Numbers above, there are certain operators and functions you can use in Python on Strings.

You can use + sign to concatenate two strings. See below:

```
In [10]: str1 = 'bob'
         str2 = 'met'
         str3 = 'sarah'
         print (str1+" "+str2+" "+str3)
         bob met sarah
```

You can also change strings to upper and lower case using upper() and lower() functions in Python and you can use count() function to determine number of characters in a string. See below:

```
In [11]: str1.upper()
Out[11]: 'BOB'

In [12]: str1.lower()
Out[12]: 'bob'

In [13]: str1.count('b')
Out[13]: 2
```

Another useful function is the replace() that lets you replace one character with another in a string. See below:

```
In [14]: str1.replace('o','r')
Out[14]: 'brb'
```

4. Data Structures

Now that we have learned about data types in Python, let's go over how Python organizes these data types into different types of data structures. We will cover the following data structures in this book:

1) Tuples
2) Lists
3) Dictionaries
4) Sets
5) Custom Objects

4.1 Tuples

Tuples are ordered sequences of data represented as data contained within parenthesis separated by commas. For example:

(1, 'two', 3.5, False)

As you can see from the above example, Tuples can contain data of all types at the same time.

Tuples are immutable – as in data within Tuples cannot be changed. For example, look at this sequence of code:

```
In [2]: tuple1 = (1,'two', 3.5, False)
        tuple1[2]=4

        ---------------------------------------------------------------------------
        TypeError                                 Traceback (most recent call last)
        <ipython-input-2-07bc96c26839> in <module>
              1 tuple1 = (1,'two', 3.5, False)
        ----> 2 tuple1[2]=4

        TypeError: 'tuple' object does not support item assignment
```

Python throws an error when we tried to assign the value of 4 to the second index in the tuple, indicating that tuples objects do not support item assignment.

Tuples can also contain other data structures like tuples – this concept is defined as 'nesting'. Imagine visualizing it as a tree as follows:

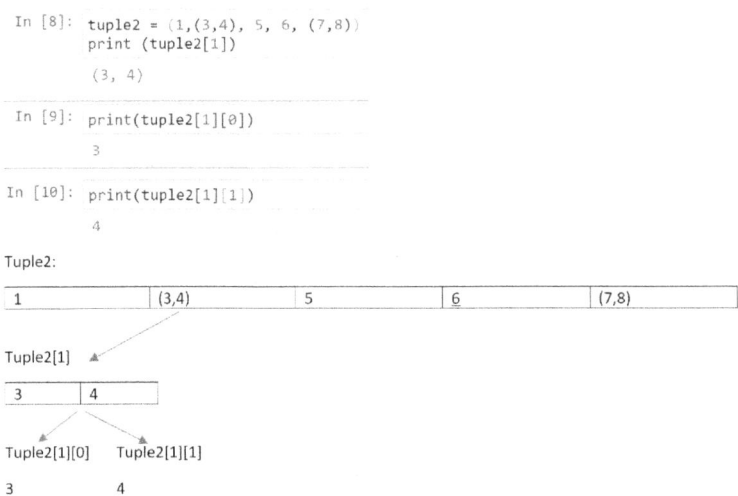

4.2 Lists

Lists are also sequenced data structures with data represented as separated by brackets (as opposed to parenthesis for tuples). For example:

[1, 'two', 3.5, False]

Unlike tuples, lists are mutable i.e. data in lists can be changed. See the following sequence of code:

```
In [11]:  list1 = [1,'two', 3.5, False]
          list1[2]=4
          print(list1)
```

[1, 'two', 4, False]

Python allows us to change the list by replacing the value 3.5 with 4 in index 2 position and does not throw an error like in the case of tuples.

Just like tuples, lists can hold multiple data types at the same time including other data structures like tuples and lists i.e. nesting as outlined above.

4.3 Dictionaries

Dictionaries are like tuples and lists in that they help order and sequence the data. However, the main difference is that they are represented by data separated by commas in curly braces and the index for dictionaries can be string labels. See code example below:

{'leader':'Abraham Lincoln', 'fighter':'Mike Tyson', 'city':'Toronto'}

In the case of dictionaries, the index or keys are immutable i.e. cannot be changed. However, the values represented by the labels can be changed. See the code sample below:

```
In [17]: dictionary1 = {'leader' : 'Abraham Lincoln', 'fighter':'Mike Tyson', 'city':'Toronto'}
         dictionary1['leader']='Winston Churchill'
         print(dictionary1)
```

{'leader': 'Winston Churchill', 'fighter': 'Mike Tyson', 'city': 'Toronto'}

In the above example, Python allows us to change the leader in the dictionary to Winston Churchill – and we used the string 'leader' as our index as opposed to 0 to access the first data element in the structure.

4.4 Sets

Sets are another example of data structures like tuples, lists and dictionaries – the key difference being that sets are not ordered i.e. they do not have indexes. The reason behind that is that the sets only contain unique elements. They are represented by data elements separated by commas in curly brackets. See code example below:

```
In [19]: set1 = {1,'two', 3.5, 3.5, False}
         print(set1)
```

{'two', 1, 3.5, False}

In the above example, even though 3.5 was duplicated in the curly brackets, when the set was created, the duplicates were removed.

Sets can have values added or removed from them using 'add' and 'remove' functions. See code example below:

```
In [24]: set1.add('twenty')
         print(set1)
         {False, 1, 3.5, 'twenty', 'two'}

In [25]: set1.remove('two')
         print(set1)
         {False, 1, 3.5, 'twenty'}
```

You can also perform additional mathematical functions on sets by showing the common elements in two sets by using the '&' function. See code example below:

```
In [26]: set2 = {'hello', 1, 3.5, 'I', 'new'}
         set2&set1
Out[26]: {1, 3.5}
```

As you would remember, set1 had data elements 1 and 3.5 that are also present in set2. So the '&' function found the commonality and returned the common data elements between the two sets.

Now let's try combining the two sets by using the 'union' function. See code example below:

```
In [28]: set1.union(set2)
Out[28]: {1, 3.5, False, 'I', 'hello', 'new', 'twenty'}
```

Notice how while combining the two data sets, Python consolidated the common elements 1 and 3.5 and did not repeat them – as duplicates are not allowed in sets.

4.5 Custom Objects

While tuples, lists, dictionaries and sets are built in data structures in Python, sometimes you may find the need to create custom objects or data structures in Python with their own attributes. Suppose you wanted to create a custom object in Python called 'Human' with its own specific attributes for re-usability in your code. Consider this code sample:

```
In [30]: #defining the custom class Human
         class Human (object ):
             def __init__ (self, height, weight):
                 self.height = height;
                 self.weight = weight;

In [31]: #initializing a Human custom class object
         newHuman = Human (60,180)
         print (newHuman.height)
         print (newHuman.weight)
         60
         180
```

Notice the following in the above lines of code:

- Custom class Human was initialized using the def key word and the '__init__' initialization function (notice the two underscores on each side of the init keyword)
- In the initialization function, 'self' is an instance of the object being created along with the two attributes 'height' and 'weight' that define the human object in this instance
- After the custom class has been defined, we use that to initialize a new Human object and pass it the

attribute values for height (60 inches) and weight (180 pounds).
- When we print out the results the object attributes assigned, we get the desired output

5. Data Traversing

Now that we have introduced different types of data structures in Python, let's see how we navigate and traverse through them. We can do so in the following ways:

1) If then else statements
2) Loops
3) Functions

5.1 If Then Else Statements

We will start with if then else statements. These conditional structures are a common presence in all object-oriented programming languages. They make use of Boolean operators introduced earlier in this book and depending on the outcome of the Boolean condition, the path forward is defined. Consider this sample of code:

```
In [2]:  wizard = 'Gandalf'
         if (wizard=='Sauron'):
             print ("oh no")
         else:
             print ("keep going")

         keep going
```

In the above example, we set the wizard variable to String value of 'Gandalf'. We then used the Boolean equals operator (==) to check if the wizard value is 'Sauron' instead. Clearly the result of that condition will be false, so Python will not print "oh no" and instead it picks the else path and prints "keep going".

In the syntax, notice how there is a colon at the end of both if and else lines of code. Also, notice how the dependent output is indented to show dependency on the if and else conditions.

Now, what if you wanted to have multiple if conditions in your code? Check out this sample of code:

```
In [18]: wizard = 'Sauron'
         elf = 'Frodo'
         helpComing = True
         if (wizard=='Sauron') and (elf=='Frodo'):
             print ("oh no")
         elif (helpComing):
             print ("keep going")
         else:
             print ("world is ending")

oh no
```

Notice that we changed the wizard variable to 'Sauron' now and we also introduced a new elf variable 'Frodo'. We have also added to the if condition by using the Boolean operator AND – basically checking if both the wizard == Sauron and elf == Frodo conditions are true. Since that is the case, Python prints "oh no" and skips the remaining conditions in the code.

What happens if we change the elf to 'Sam'? Let's find out:

```
In [19]:  wizard = 'Sauron'
          elf = 'Sam'
          helpComing = True
          if (wizard=='Sauron') and (elf=='Frodo'):
              print ("oh no")
          elif (helpComing):
              print ("keep going")
          else:
              print ("world is ending")

          keep going
```

Since our first if condition is dependent on wizard being 'Sauron' and elf being 'Frodo', it is no longer true. So Python skips that condition and goes to the condition branch elif (short for else if). We know that helpComing is set to True, so Python will print "keep going" as the output.

5.2 Loops

Just like if then else statements, for loops and while loops are a common presence in object-oriented programming languages.

For loops are used to traverse data structures based on specific conditions. See code example below:

```
In [10]:  list1 = [1,3,5,7,9]
          for i,list in enumerate (list1):
              list1[i]=list+1
          print (list1)

          [2, 4, 6, 8, 10]
```

In the above example, we started with a list of odd numbers and we wanted to convert them to even numbers. We start out with using the 'enumerate' function in Python which essentially produces the index for each data element in the list. We then iterate through the list by assigning the index to i variable and adding 1 to each element in the list until we are done going through the entire list as follows:

list [0] = 1+1 = 2

list [1] = 3+1 = 4

list [3] = 5+1 = 6

and so on...

The outcome is a list of even numbers: [2, 4, 6, 8, 10]. Remember earlier in the book we mentioned that, lists are mutable and that's why we were able to change the odd numbers to even numbers in the list – this function will not have worked for tuples which are immutable.

Now let's try traversing a set – if you recall, sets are shown in curly braces and do not have indices. So what do we do in that case? Not to worry, Python has an answer for that as well. Check out this sample code:

```
In [17]: set1 = {'one','two','three','four'}
         for set in set1:
             print (set + ' mississippi')
         
         two mississippi
         three mississippi
         four mississippi
         one mississippi
```

Notice how without using an index, Python assigns the value of each data element to the set variable and lets you iterate through the entire length of the set? That's the elegance and simplicity of Python!

Now let's look at another example of loops in Python – while loops. While loops are great for traversing data structures where the size of the data structures is not known, and you would like to traverse until a specific condition is met. Consider this sample code:

```
In [23]: i = 0
         metals = ['silver', 'copper', 'iron', 'gold','bronze','diamond']
         while (metals[i] != 'gold'):
             print ('hop ' + str(i))
             i = i+1
         print ("found gold!")
hop 0
hop 1
hop 2
found gold!
```

In the above example, we were trying to find 'gold' but don't know how many hops it will take to hit gold. So, we set our index to 0 and set the Boolean condition in the while loop to keep going while the metal is not equal to gold. We finally find gold after 3 total hops and end the loop before hitting 'bronze' or 'diamond' which are later in the list.

5.3 Functions

In Python, you have the option to define your own functions if there is specific set of operations you expect to repeat on a data structure. For example, suppose you always wanted to return multiples of a specific number anytime a list of numeric values is provided to you. You can define a function as follows:

In [24]:
```python
# defining the function multiples
def multiples (x, list1):
    for i,list in enumerate (list1):
        list1[i]=list*x
    return list1
# trying the function multiples
list1 = [13, 15, 17, 19]
multiples (4,list1)
print (list1)
```

[52, 60, 68, 76]

In the above example, we defined a function called 'multiples' using the def keyword in Python. We define the function as taking two parameters 'x' – that being the number that we will multiply the list with and 'list1' – that being the list we will convert to multiples of x.

Once we are done defining the function, we try it out by passing it a list of values of 13, 15, 17 and 19 and ask the multiples function to convert the list by multiplying it by 4. The outcome is 52, 60, 68 and 76 – all multiples of 4 as desired. Now you can re-use this custom defined function later in your code as well – as required.

6. Data Exploration and Analysis

Now that we have covered different data types, structures and how to use them, we will take it one step further and cover how we work with data files and data frames. We will also introduce two foundational Python libraries: Pandas and Numpy.

For the purposes of this and upcoming chapters, we will use a sample fictional dataset that contains house sales prices based on various house features such as:

1) Year Built – Year house was built
2) Square Footage – Size of the house in square feet
3) House Type – Whether the house is a detached, semi-detached or townhouse
4) Garage Size – Number of cars that the garage can accommodate
5) Fireplaces – Whether house has a fireplace or not
6) Pool – Whether house has a pool or not
7) Sale Price – Actual sale price of the house based on the above features

You can download this sample dataset as a .csv file from my website by following this link:
https://www.daneyalauthor.com

6.1 Explore and Clean Data with Pandas

Now that we have selected our dataset to work with, let's first start with reading the train.csv file that we downloaded earlier. For that we will use a built in Python library called 'Pandas'. Pandas are cute furry animals but in Python they also allow us to work with data as organized data frames. This library also has built in functions that we can perform on these data frames. We start with importing this library as follows:

```
import pandas as pd
```

Here we have used the import keyword to create an instance of pandas to process the house sales data and named it 'pd'. We now import the House Sales Values.csv file as follows:

```
#Importing data from House Sales csv file into a panda dataframe
df = pd.read_csv('House Sales Values.csv')
```

In the above code sample, we used the pandas function 'read_csv' by passing it the path to the train.csv file and stored it into our data frame called 'df'.

We are now ready to use pandas' data exploratory functions, so we can understand our dataset better.

Let's start by looking at the first 10 records of the data set. For that we use the pandas head() function. See code sample below:

```
#Having a look at first 10 rows of our dataset
print ("Print first 10 rows of dataset")
print (df.head(10))
```

```
Print first 10 rows of dataset
   YearBuilt  SquareFootage HouseType  NumCarGarage Fireplaces Pool  SalePrice
0       2002           3201      Semi           4.0        Yes   No  2000000.0
1       2017           3150      Semi           3.0        Yes   No  2000000.0
2       2000           2455  Detached           3.0         No   No   400000.0
3       2006           2560      Semi           4.0        Yes   No   400000.0
4       2005           3415       NaN           2.0         No  Yes  2000000.0
5       2015           3654      Town           3.0         No   No  2000000.0
6       2015           2071      Town           4.0         No   No   400000.0
7       2004           1310      Town           1.0        Yes  Yes   750000.0
8       2019           2646  Detached           1.0         No   No   400000.0
9       2001           1191      Town           2.0         No   No   750000.0
```

Note that in the above code sample, we passed 10 as an argument to the head() function. If we had passed 20 as an argument e.g. df.head(20), Python would have returned first 20 rows.

Let's also have a look at how many rows and columns our dataset has, using the pandas shape attribute. See code sample below:

```
#Looking at shape of our dataframe
print ("Shape of our dataset")
print (df.shape)
```

```
Shape of our dataset
(1000, 7)
```

Looks like our dataset has 1000 rows and 7 columns. Ok great, now let's find out what are data types in each column of the data frame. For that we will use the pandas dtypes attribute. See code sample below:

```
#Looking at data types in our data set
print ("Data types in our dataset")
print (df.dtypes)
```

```
Data types in our dataset
YearBuilt            int64
SquareFootage        int64
HouseType            object
NumCarGarage         float64
Fireplaces           object
Pool                 object
SalePrice            float64
dtype: object
```

Looks like we have a mix of integers, floats and strings (objects) in our dataset. Good to know and this will come in handy as we transform our data for further processing later in this book.

Let's further describe this data set using the describe() function to understand it better. See code sample below:

```
#Describing our dataset
print ("Descrbing our dataset")
print (df.describe())
```

```
Descrbing our dataset
         YearBuilt    SquareFootage    NumCarGarage       SalePrice
count   1000.000000    1000.000000      999.000000     9.950000e+02
mean    2009.567000    2484.388000        2.487487     1.025226e+06
std        5.934368     857.178259        1.142894     6.778931e+05
min     2000.000000    1000.000000        1.000000     4.000000e+05
25%     2004.000000    1771.250000        1.000000     4.000000e+05
50%     2009.000000    2466.500000        2.000000     7.500000e+05
75%     2015.000000    3229.250000        4.000000     2.000000e+06
max     2019.000000    3992.000000        4.000000     2.000000e+06
```

The describe function gave us additional important statistics on our dataset – for example what is the count, mean, max and min values for different numeric features like Year Built, Square Footage, Car Garage Size and Sale Price of the house.

Ok now let's clean this data before processing it further. Let's find out how many null values we have for each column.

```
#find out total count of data
total_count = df.isnull().sum().sort_values(ascending=False)

#find out percent missing data relative to full data set
percent_missing = (df.isnull().sum()/df_train.isnull().count()).sort_values(ascending=False)
missing_data = pd.concat([total_count, percent_missing], axis=1, keys=['Total', 'Percent'])
missing_data.head(20)
```

	Total	Percent
HouseType	10	0.010
Pool	6	0.006
SalePrice	5	0.005
Fireplaces	3	0.003
NumCarGarage	1	0.001
SquareFootage	0	0.000
YearBuilt	0	0.000

Looks like for certain columns, a small percentage of data is null. For example, House Type is missing in 10 records and Sale Price is missing in 5 records. As this amount of missing data will introduce discrepancies in our analysis, we will drop these columns for simplicity and re-shape and describe our data set. See code sample below:

```
#Removing null values in our data set and re-checking shape
df.dropna(axis=0, inplace=True)

#Updated of our dataframe
print ("Updated shape of our dataset")
print (df.shape)
```

```
Updated shape of our dataset
(980, 7)
```

We now have a smaller data set to work with, consisting of 980 rows, 7 columns and no null values!

6.2 Find Outliers with Numpy and Scipy

Before we go further though, let's introduce a few more foundational libraries in Python.

1) **Numpy** is a library that is used for performing numeric operations on data structures like lists and matrices
2) **Scipy** is a library that leverages Numpy data structures for advanced algebra and calculus operations
3) **Scikit-learn (also known as Sklearn)** is a foundational Python library for building predictive models

To leverage the numeric calculations (Numpy), statistical analysis (Scipy) and predictive modeling (Scikit-learn) functions in the above libraries, we need to replace categorical string values in our dataset with numeric values. Since this is a common issue, Sklearn library has built-in functions that allow you to do exactly that in very few lines of code. See below:

```python
from sklearn.preprocessing import LabelEncoder

#get all categorical features
categorical_cols = ['HouseType','Fireplaces','Pool']
print('name of categorical features')
print(categorical_cols)
print("number of categorical features = ",len(categorical_cols))

#convert categorical variables into labels
labelEncoder = LabelEncoder()

#applying the label encoder to the categorical features
for categorical_col in categorical_cols:
    df[categorical_col] = labelEncoder.fit_transform(df[categorical_col])

print("all categorical features converted successfully")

#Having a look at first 10 rows of our dataset
print ("Print first 10 rows of dataset")
print (df.head(10))

#Looking at data types in our data set
print ("Data types in our dataset")
print (df.dtypes)
```

In the above code snapshot, we completed the following steps:

1) We created an array of column names with non-numeric (Boolean or String) values – House Type, Fireplaces and Pool
2) We then used the LabelEncoder() function in Scikit-learn library to transform all the non-numeric columns to numeric values – essentially replacing string values with numeric codes like 0, 1, 2. Notice how we used the for loop introduced earlier in this book to traverse this data structure
3) We then print out the first 10 rows of our dataset and as well as data types. See below:

```
name of categorical features
['HouseType', 'Fireplaces', 'Pool']
number of categorical features =  3
all categorical features converted successfully
Print first 10 rows of dataset
    YearBuilt  SquareFootage  HouseType  NumCarGarage  Fireplaces  Pool  \
0       2002           3201          1           4.0           1     0
1       2017           3150          1           3.0           1     0
2       2000           2455          0           3.0           0     0
3       2006           2560          1           4.0           1     0
5       2015           3654          2           3.0           0     0
6       2015           2071          2           4.0           0     0
7       2004           1310          2           1.0           1     1
8       2019           2646          0           1.0           0     0
9       2001           1191          2           2.0           0     0
10      2016           3279          2           4.0           0     0

     SalePrice
0   2000000.0
1   2000000.0
2    400000.0
3    400000.0
5   2000000.0
6    400000.0
7    750000.0
8    400000.0
9    750000.0
10  2000000.0
```

Notice how for Fireplaces and Pool, before we had 'Yes' and 'No' values and they have now been replaced with 1 and 0 respectively. Also, for House Type different house types have been re-coded as follows 0, 1, 2.

Our data types for different columns in the dataset are also numeric:

```
Data types in our dataset
YearBuilt         int64
SquareFootage     int64
HouseType         int64
NumCarGarage      float64
Fireplaces        int64
Pool              int64
SalePrice         float64
dtype: object
```

We will use Numpy and SciPy libraries to find outliers in our data set to clean it further. For that we will use Z-score method.

Z-score basically indicates how far from the mean a data point is. Typically, a Z-score of 3 or more is a good indicator of an outlier. Let's look for these outliers in our data set.

```python
#Import Numpy library
import numpy as np

#Import Scipy library
from scipy import stats

#Calculate z scores
z_scores = np.abs(stats.zscore(df))

#Narrow down data set to all columns with z scores of less than 3
df = df[(z_scores < 3).all(axis=1)]
print ("data frame with no outliers shape", df.shape)
print ("data frame with no outliers describe", df.describe())
```

In the above code, we followed the following steps to calculate and remove our outliers:

1) We imported Numpy and Scipy libraries
2) We then calculated Z scores for each of the numeric values in our data frame using the Scipy stats.zscore function
3) We then re-formed the data frame with data that has Z score of less than 3 to eliminate all the outliers
4) Finally, we printed out the shape of this updated data set

```
data frame with no outliers shape (980, 7)
data frame with no outliers describe          YearBuilt  SquareFootage  HouseType  NumCarGarage  Fireplaces \
count    980.000000    980.000000   980.000000   980.000000     980.000000
mean    2009.425510   2490.789796     1.028571     2.497959       0.513265
std        5.849977    868.731111     0.825537     1.108513       0.500079
min     2000.000000   1007.000000     0.000000     1.000000       0.000000
25%     2004.000000   1741.750000     0.000000     1.000000       0.000000
50%     2009.000000   2493.500000     1.000000     3.000000       1.000000
75%     2015.000000   3252.250000     2.000000     3.000000       1.000000
max     2019.000000   3995.000000     2.000000     4.000000       1.000000

              Pool      SalePrice
count   980.000000   9.800000e+02
mean      0.467347   1.151014e+06
std       0.499187   4.930919e+05
min       0.000000   3.004030e+05
25%       0.000000   7.154208e+05
50%       0.000000   1.159595e+06
75%       1.000000   1.569744e+06
max       1.000000   1.996401e+06
```

Good news! Z-Score function did not find any outliers and our dataset still has the same size – 980 rows and 7 columns.

6.3 Visualize Data with Matplotlib and Seaborn

Now that we have removed all null values, replaced string values and checked for outliers, let's find out which features of the house have the biggest impact on house sales price. Easiest way to see that is by visualizing your data. For that we will use two additional Python libraries:

1) **Matplotlib** is the foundational library for creating graphs and plots in Python
2) **Seaborn** is a more advanced data visualization library and is based on the Matplotlib as its foundation

Let's use the above two libraries to visualize our data and see which features impact the house sale prices the most. We will first look at the distribution of the house sale prices as follows:

```
#Let's visualize our data to look at how sale price is distributed
import matplotlib.pyplot as plt
import seaborn as sns

print ("Overall Sale Price distribution")
sns.distplot(df['SalePrice']);
```
Overall Sale Price distribution

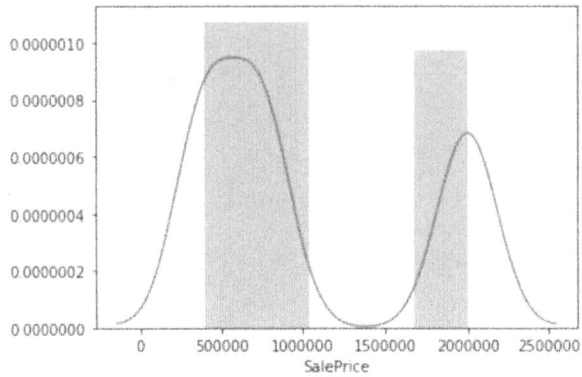

In the above snapshot, we covered the following steps:

1) We first imported the matplotlib and seaborn libraries
2) We then called the distribution plot function called 'distplot' and passed it the Sale Price column to generate the distribution plot visualization

The distribution plot shows us that that the sale prices range between $500,000 to $1 million and then $2 million.

Now, let's create a new data visualization called box plots – to see house prices by different house types. As you may recall, we re-coded the house types in the previous chapter as follows:

House Type – String Value	House Type – Numeric Encoding

Detached	0
Semi-Detached	1
Town-home	2

Let's see how we generate a box plot visualization using the following code:

```
var = 'HouseType'
data = pd.concat([df['SalePrice'], df[var]], axis=1)
f, ax = plt.subplots(figsize=(14, 8))
fig = sns.boxplot(x=var, y="SalePrice", data=data)
fig.axis(ymin=300000, ymax=2000000);
```

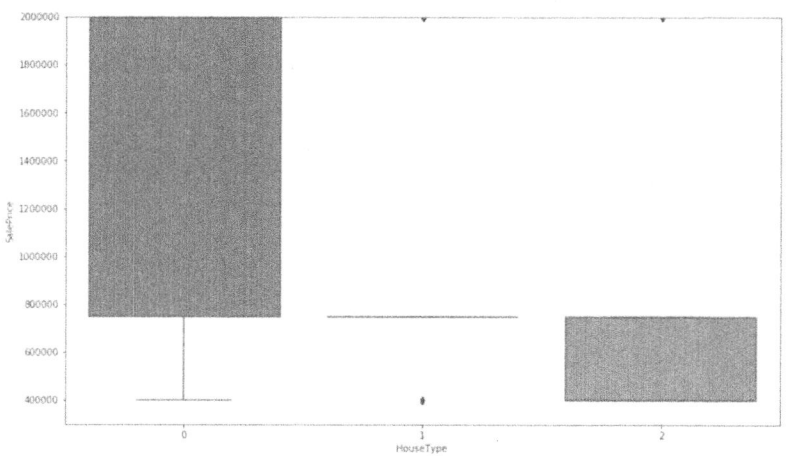

Based on the above visual, we see that detached house prices can range from $800,000 to $2,000,000, semi-detached houses are just below the $800,000 mark and townhomes are in the $400,000 to under $800,000 range.

While the above visualizations give us a good idea of impact of individual variables on the house sales price, it is even better to be able to see the relative impact of all variables on the house sales price.

For that we will use the correlation matrix and heatmap visualization – see snapshot below:

```
#correlation matrix
correlation_matrix = df.corr()
f, ax = plt.subplots(figsize=(20, 10))
sns.heatmap(correlation_matrix, cmap="YlGnBu", vmax=.9, square=True);
```

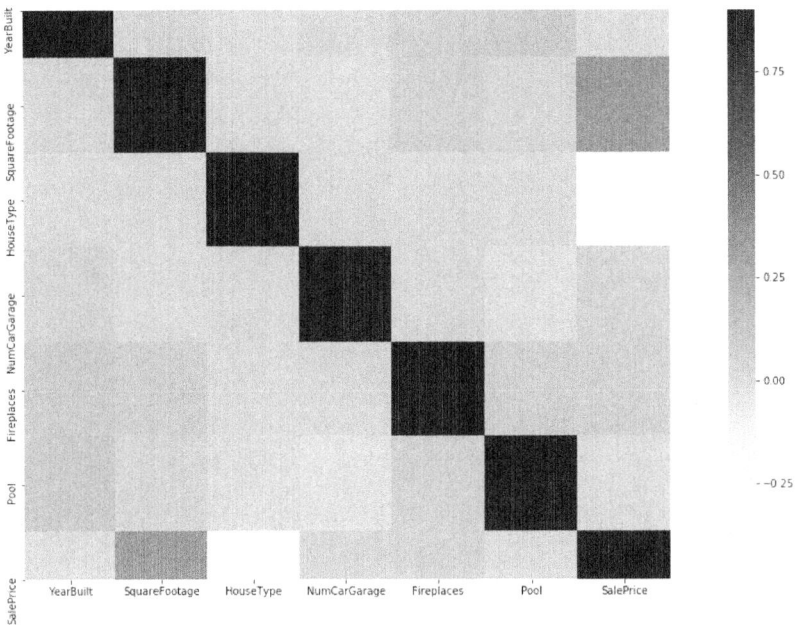

From the above heatmap, we can see that Square Footage and House Type are the two distinctive features that have a material impact on the house sales price (based on their distinctive colors on the gradient scale on the right).

7. Building Predictive Models

Now that we have selected a dataset and cleaned it for null values and outliers, we are ready to build different predictive models. But what is a predictive model? In the simplest terms, predictive models use the past to predict the future. They analyze current state factors, correlations and data relationships to determine how things will play out based on these dependences.

We will build two different kind of predictive models in this chapter using the dataset we have been working with so far:

1) Linear Regression
2) Decision Tree Regression

We will then test and compare the accuracy of these predictive models.

Regression: Before we go too far, we just mentioned a new term – regression. Why would predictive models, that predict the future, be referencing regression? Regression is a statistical technique and the term was first used by Francis Galton ([6]) in 1877 when describing how the heights of descendants tended to regress towards the mean as opposed to increasing with each new generation. This term then evolved into the statistical concept of describing the relationship between dependent variables like house sale price and independent variables like house square footage and number of garages.

There is a wide variety of different machine learning and predictive algorithms and I will go over some of them at a higher level in the next chapter. However, I will go over in more detail why Linear Regression and Decision Tree are suitable algorithms for this specific problem.

To train our models, we will first split our data into train and test data sets as per below:

```
#Splitting our data into train and test sets
from sklearn.model_selection import train_test_split

X = df.drop('SalePrice', axis=1)
y = df['SalePrice']

X_train , X_test , y_train , y_test = train_test_split(X,y,test_size=0.50, random_state=80, shuffle =True)
print('Data split successfully in training and test data sets')
```

In the above code sample, we used the train_test_split function in the Scikit-learn library. As you can see, we defined 'y' as the target / dependent variable 'SalePrice' and 'X' as all the independent variables that will be used to predict the price.

We will take a moment here to describe the purpose of the additional parameters in the train_test_split function:

1) test_size – defines what percentage of your data will be treated as test dataset. For this example, we used 50%
2) random_state – is used as an input into random number generation during the split. For our example, we used 80
3) shuffle – is used to determine whether data should be shuffled before splitting. For our purpose, we set that to true

Now we are ready to build, train and test the predictive models!

7.1 Linear Regression Model

A linear regression model assumes a linear relationship between a dependent or target variable e.g. Sale Price for the house and independent variables like square footage, number of garages etc.

It can be illustrated as an equation as follows:

Y = cX + I

Where

Y = dependent variable aka Sale Price of the House

X = independent variable e.g. Square footage

c = coefficient – that will be calculated by the linear regression model

I = intercept – that will be calculated by the linear regression model as well

The above is a case of Simple Linear Regression, where you only have one dependent and one independent variables.

When you have multiple independent variables, like in our case, we use the equation below and this can be defined as Multiple Linear Regression

Y = I+ (c1X1)+ (c2X2)+ (c3X3)+......

We can initialize, train and test the Linear Regression Model as follows:

```
#Building and Testing Linear Regression Model
from sklearn.linear_model import LinearRegression

#Initializing the Linear Regression Model
LR = LinearRegression(copy_X=True)
LR.fit(X_train,y_train)
print("Linear regression model trained successfully")

#Making a prediction using the test data in the Linear Regression Model
yhat = LR.predict(X_test)

#Two ways to measure the accuracy of the Linear Regression Model
#1) Mean Squared Error (MSE) that calculates the difference between actual and predicted values as follows
from sklearn.metrics import mean_squared_error
print ("Mean squared error of Linear Regression Model", mean_squared_error(y_test, yhat))

#2) R-squared also known as coefficient of determination that calculates how close is the data to the fitted regression line
print ("R squared error of Linear Regression Model on Training Data", LR.score (X_train, y_train))
print ("R squared error of Linear Regression Model on Testing Data", LR.score (X_test, y_test))

Linear regression model trained successfully
Mean squared error of Linear Regression Model 280817720691.3239
R squared error of Linear Regression Model on Training Data 0.2818905399647811
R squared error of Linear Regression Model on Testing Data 0.3881160275230543
```

In the above code snapshot, we covered the following steps:

1) We initialized the Linear Regression Model from the Scikit-Learn library
2) We then fit (or trained) the model using the training data set
3) We made the prediction using the test data set
4) We tested the accuracy of the model using two methods:
    a. Mean Squared Error (MSE) – that calculates the difference between actual and predicted values
    b. R-Squared (also known as co-efficient of determination) – that calculates how close is the data to the fitted regression line. Or to say it simply, how well does our model 'fit' the data. R-squared is on a scale of 0 to 1 and a negative score typically indicates an issue with the model fit. In our case, we got around an R-squared value of .39 for the test data. That means roughly 39% of the variation in

house sale prices is due to the variation in the independent variables like square footage and house type we identified earlier

7.2 Decision Tree Regression Model

Now let's try a different kind of predictive model algorithm called decision tree. Why would we want to use this type of algorithm to predict house sale prices?

A decision tree regression model forms a tree structure as it breaks down the dataset into smaller subsets and keeps traversing down different nodes to arrive at a prediction. In case of house sales prices, a decision tree can be visualized as follows:

The above is an overly simplified illustration of the decision tree on how the model will arrive at a sale price prediction but it gets the point across.

Below is how we will initiate, train, test and evaluate a Decision Tree Regression model in Python.

```python
from sklearn.tree import DecisionTreeRegressor

# Initializing the Decision Tree Regression Model
saleTree = DecisionTreeRegressor(random_state = 100)

# fit the regressor with X and Y data
saleTree.fit(X_train, y_train)
print("Decision tree regression model trained successfully")

#Making a prediction using the test data in the Decision Tree Regression Model
predTree = saleTree.predict(X_test)

from sklearn import metrics
print("DecisionTrees's Accuracy: ", metrics.accuracy_score(y_test, predTree))
```

```
Decision tree regression model trained successfully
DecisionTrees's Accuracy:  0.6693877551020408
```

The above is a very basic illustration of how you would initialize a Decision Tree Regression model. In the above sample code, we covered the following steps:

1) We initialized the Decision Tree Regression Model from the Scikit-Learn library
2) We then fit (or trained) the model using the training data set
3) We made the prediction using the test data set
4) We tested the accuracy of the model using the metrics.accuracy_score function in the Scikit-Learn library and got an accuracy score of 67% - that is an improvement over the Linear Regression model result we got earlier

Typically finding the best fitting model for your dataset is a trial and error exercise and we work with the one that is giving us the highest degree of accuracy based on our training and test datasets.

8. Understanding Machine Learning

In the previous chapter, I described two machine learning models: Linear Regression and Decision Tree analysis. I also mentioned that there are many other machine learning models that can be applied based on the nature of the problem at hand. In this chapter, we will explain additional machine learning models and algorithms in simple terms – with a goal for the reader to be able to understand them at a high level and know when to apply them given the nature of the data and their data science use case.

At the highest level, machine learning models can be classified into three categories:

1) Supervised Machine Learning Models
2) Unsupervised Machine Learning Models
3) Deep Learning Models

8.1 Supervised Machine Learning Models

In case of supervised machine learning models, the model is provided some direction in terms of how to classify the data and it uses those instructions to learn before making its predictions. In the house sales example that we used in the previous chapter, that was an example of supervised learning as we told the model what the different types of houses were and even which house features have an impact on the sales price. We then split the data set into training and test sets, that the model used to make its prediction.

Examples of supervised machine learning models include:

1) Regression analysis
2) Classification analysis

Regression analysis – in case of regression analysis, given several factors, the model is expected to predict a number. In case of the house sales price example, the model considered several house features to predict the house sales price. Note that above was an example of **linear regression** where there is a straight-line correlation between dependent variable (e.g. house sales price) and independent variables (e.g. house type, number of garages etc.).

There are certainly situations where that straight-line correlation does not exist and typically in those situations, **polynomial regression** analysis is used – or a curved line instead of a straight line.

In other words, all the machine learning model is doing when performing regression analysis is it is trying to fit a line between scattered data points to find a correlation between independent and dependent variables. That can be illustrated visually as follows:

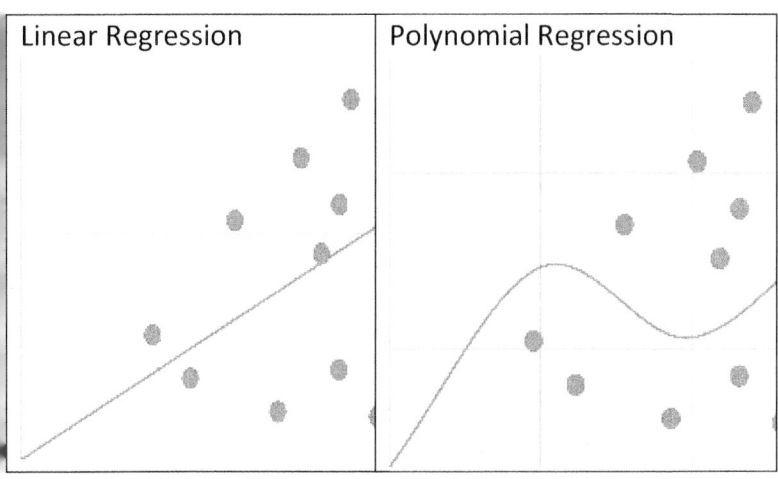

Other real-world examples of where regression analysis is used is in the finance industry predicting stock price based on historical and market trends as well as in the retail industry where certain product prices are often predictable based on seasonality and time of the year e.g. clothing, outdoor patio and gardening products.

Classification analysis – in case of classification analysis, the machine learning model predicts the category for an object based on its features. So the main difference between classification model and regression model is that the classification model is categorizing the objects and regression model is predicting a number associated with an object.

Like regression analysis, since classification analysis is a supervised model, it will need to be provided labeled data with instructions to learn before it can make its predictions.

If house sales data example in the previous chapter was a classification problem, the model would have been given house sales data without the house type and model would have been asked to predict the house type (e.g. detached, semi-detached or townhome) based on the different features included in the dataset.

Other real-world examples where classification algorithm can be used include:

1) Classifying insurance applicant into different risk categories based on their health data
2) Categorizing call center calls as potential escalations, based language and sentiment used
3) Categorizing incoming emails based on specific parameters

8.2 Unsupervised Machine Learning Models

Unsupervised models are basically like intelligent but unsupervised children – who are given a whole bunch of data but without a lot of direction or labelling of the data. The models then assess this data and draw conclusions. These conclusions continue to be refined as more data is provided to the model.

Examples of unsupervised machine learning models include:

1) Clustering
2) Dimension Reduction
3) Association Learning

Clustering is, as the name suggests, like classification model above where it defines clusters of similar objects but the main difference being that the model is not given any pre-defined categories to label the data with. It comes up with them on its own. As an example, imagine the model being asked to classify different kinds of unlabeled data – some data loosely fits in the time category, some data fits in the geographical category and some data is not fitting either of these dimensions and instead is grouped in the general data cluster as illustrated below:

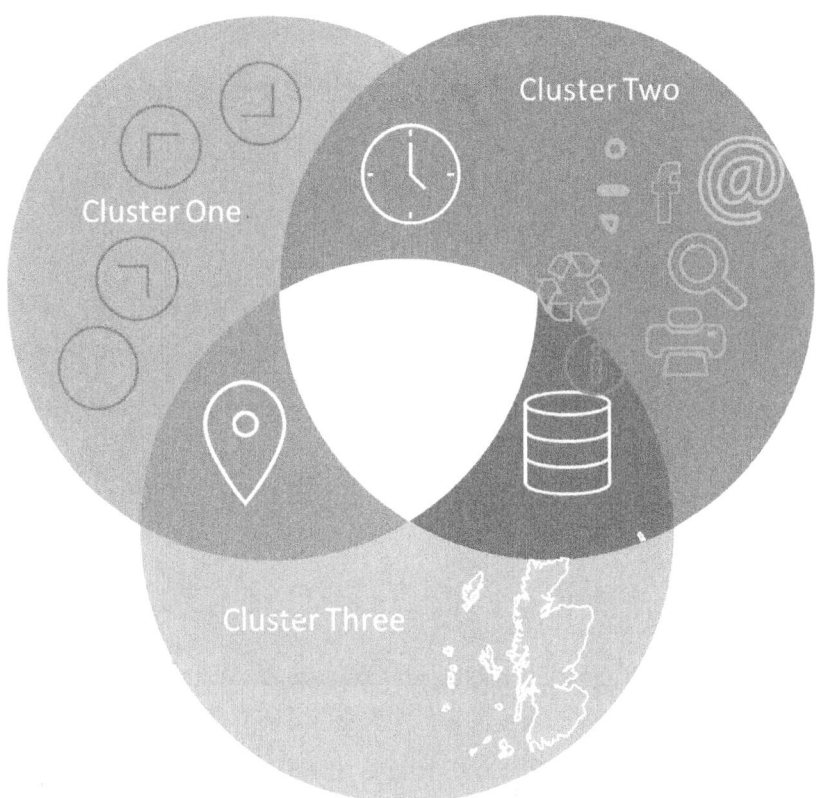

Real-world examples of clustering include detecting anomalies in cancer research based on cancerous cell properties as well as fraud detection based on irregular insurance claims or financial investment patterns in case of money laundering.

K-means algorithms is a popular algorithm in Python that is an example of clustering. Basically the algorithm finds its nearest K neighbors that have similar properties – with K defining the number of neighbors you are pre-setting the model to find.

Dimension Reduction is another example of unsupervised machine learning model that takes a set of features of different objects and tries to categorize them to a higher degree of categories. Think of Netflix algorithm to classify incoming movies and TV shows – it typically will roll up the different types of content to several high-level categories automatically like action, horror or comedy. As new content gets added to the platform, the algorithm will further refine itself to cluster the movies more accurately. In certain cases, certain content on Netflix may fit multiple clusters. For example, a vampire movie with a lot of action can likely be in both the action and horror clusters.

Association Learning is a more sophisticated form of unsupervised machine learning model that is learning from customer behavior and recommending new products and services to you based on your prior purchasing habits. These types of systems are often called recommender systems that associate client profile with the product clusters and based on that generate recommendations. To extend the Netflix example, once the model has built clusters of different online viewable content, it associates the content with your prior viewing habits and recommends new movies and tv shows to you that fit the categories you most often watch. The same logic applies to when Amazon recommends new books or products to you each time you login.

8.3 Deep Learning

If you have ever heard the terms machine learning and deep learning interchangeably, I am here to tell you that they are not the same. Deep learning is an advanced form of machine learning where you combine several machine learning models in a network, often called a neural network, to arrive at a final conclusion or decision.

The reason why it is called 'deep learning', is based on how deep the neural network goes or how many nodes are part of the network – with each node representing a decision point or recommendation from an interconnecting model.

The neural network can be made more sophisticated by applying different weighting to different decision points or nodes and this weighting gets adjusted over time as the model becomes smarter by learning from more experience, trial and error and more data provided to it. One example of this could be when you are looking for another job, when you are early in your career, you may put a higher weight on salary. However, as you gain more experience, you may start to add more weight to other aspects like work-life balance, benefits and career progression opportunities. A sample neural network is illustrated below as an example:

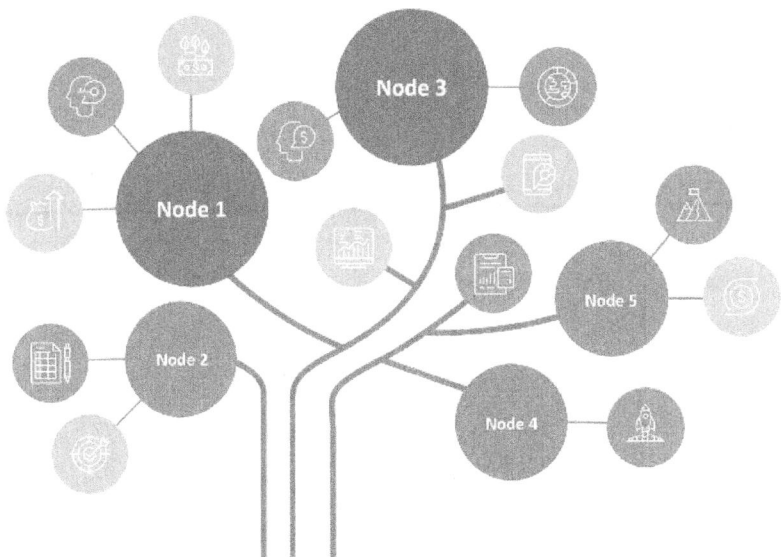

Popular deep learning Python libraries include:

1) TensorFlow
2) Keras
3) PyTorch

TensorFlow is an open source framework and API for programming deep learning neural networks and can be imported as a library in Python. It is capable of working with large data sets and is very efficient in data processing – that is why it is gaining a lot of popularity in data science and academic communities.

Keras can run on top of the TensorFlow framework but is more suitable for smaller datasets and rapid prototyping. You will see it mostly in use when you are experimenting with neural networks in development and traversing the nodes of the neural networks as part of the trial and error process in teaching the model.

PyTorch is most commonly used for natural language processing and was developed by Facebook. What is Natural Language Processing (NLP) you ask? It is a way for the machine learning models to interpret human language and process that as input into their algorithm. For example, instead of providing the model if-then-else conditions and code as in the previous chapter, you can ask the model questions in human language like, "What would be my predicted house price based on the square footage?" and the model returns the prediction after running the question through the algorithm. Think of AI devices like Amazon's Alexa and Google Home. Those are examples of Natural Language Processing.

9. How to Problem Solve Using Machine Learning

Now that we understand how to build machine learning models in Python and different kinds of machine and deep learning algorithms, how do we apply them to real world problems in our day to day lives or in our organization? In this chapter, I will go over a structured process on how you can go from an initial problem statement all the way to a machine learning model to address that problem.

As part of this framework, we will cover the following steps:

1) Establish your use case
2) Gain agreement on your project drivers: Time, Cost and Scope
3) Confirm if data is readily available
4) Confirm quality of your data
5) Confirm interpretability of your data
6) Visualize your data
7) Fit the right machine learning model to your use case
8) If your use case allows for a supervised model, train your model
9) If real world data is available, test your model's predictions against this data for accuracy
10) Productionize your model
11) Iterate!

9.1 Establish Your Use Case

This step involves formulation of your problem statement and I recommend that this problem statement should be formulated as a question that needs to be addressed or insight that needs to be gained. More specific the question is, the better. This step is particularly critical when you are trying to determine which machine learning algorithm best fits your problem. Some examples of use cases below for reference:

1) "How many call center representatives should I have managing my life insurance claim queues during downtime in the summer based on historical volumes and seasonality?"
2) "Based on the language and tone used in the call center call, how likely is this client to leave our organization or escalate the issue?"
3) "Depending on purchase pattern of this client, what additional products is he / she likely to buy in the next 6 months?"

9.2 Get Agreement on Project Drivers: Time, Cost and Scope

Once you have nailed down your problem statement, it is important to understand what constraints you are working with for your data science project.

1) If your project is time driven, it likely requires a quick resolution or incremental deliverables that need to provide immediate insights

2) If your project is cost driven, you likely will not have a lot of budget for data sourcing or additional resources
3) If your project is scope or quality driven, you have additional flexibility to truly perfect your model and corresponding predictions before the result is shared with your clients

9.3 Confirm If Data Is Readily Available

Depending on the nature of the problem, sometimes data may or may not be readily available. For example, if you are trying to analyze the patterns of the flu virus to inform efforts to create the vaccine for upcoming flu seasons, you may not have the most up to date dataset based on the current flu season – due to the timing or data being provided by the health institutions. In those cases, you must work with what is available and extrapolate / make assumptions where possible.

In a cost or time driven project, this situation will be a barrier. In the absence of actionable data, you will likely have to convince the stakeholders via a business case as to why investing in sourcing additional data to address the problem is the right investment to make.

9.4 Confirm Quality of Your Data

You can be swimming in data but it is possible that the quality of your data is not good i.e. you have a lot of missing, incomplete or generally uninterpretable information. You will have to spend a lot of time in data cleaning and manipulation before it is ready for analysis. In a lot of data science projects, this is the least sexy and most time intensive exercise.

Good news here is that Python has a lot of built in functions, as we illustrated earlier in this book that allow you to clean your data and visualize it to eliminate any outliers as well as null values.

9.5 Confirm Interpretability of Your Data

You can have lots of data of great quality. However, you will have a hard time analyzing or training the model if no one in your organization understands it. In case your parachuted into an organization to work on their data science project, it is highly likely that the organization has a lot of old legacy systems, that use their own internal encoding and knowledge of the data and how to interpret it is often in people's heads or is tribal knowledge i.e. its known to a select few old timers but is not documented or widely shared.

In an organization that is very operationally focused and cannot make data subject matter experts (SMEs) available to assist on data science projects, this is often a stumbling block. Often, availability of these SMEs must be business cased to move the data science project forward.

9.6 Visualize Your Data

Now that you have good quality data that is interpretable and you have ready access to SMEs, you are ready to analyze your data and the fun truly begins! As a first step, you visualize your data to look at patterns, anomalies and outliers.

This is also the step where you start to decide which machine learning model and algorithm is most suited to your problem and the structure of your data. For example, as shown earlier in this book, if you are seeing straight-line correlation between your variables, maybe it is a simple linear regression problem. Or maybe, it is a bunch of undefined data points and you need to find groupings and commonalities – sounds like a job for a clustering algorithm!

Luckily Python has really powerful visualization libraries like seaborn that allow you to look at your data from various angles before you decide on which model will be the best fit.

9.7 Fit the Right Machine Learning Model to Your Use Case

As mentioned above, visualization of your data along with the nature of your use case and project drivers will determine which model you will ultimately choose as your best fit. It is basically like selecting the best tool in your tool belt for the job at hand or using the best golf club depending on whether you need to drive or putt. You get the idea!

As mentioned earlier in this book and illustrated in the house sales example, often it is a trial and error process before you find the model that gives you the highest degree of accuracy when tested against real world data.

9.8 Train Your Model

In case of a supervised machine learning model, you have an opportunity to provide your model with labeled data and a training data set to get it ready for real world problems. Even in unsupervised or deep learning models, you can refine your models as more data becomes available and you can adjust your algorithm.

For example, in the house sales data we were using, we saw that house type and square footage played a big role in driving house sales prices. However, it was also a relatively small dataset. It is quite possible that as more data became available, additional house features like number of garages or whether the house has a pool may have become more important and model will have to be re-trained.

9.9 Test Your Model

It is not enough that you built your model and trained it once. You constantly have to test it and keep feeding it new data as feedback loop to make sure that the model accuracy stays within acceptable limits. It is also a best practice to have monitoring mechanisms developed so that if model accuracy or error rates are exceeding certain thresholds it is time to take the model back to the drawing board for re-training.

9.10 Productionize Your Model

If the machine learning model you built was meant for an ongoing operational setting in an organization as opposed to a one-off analysis, your final step is to operationalize and automate the model training and testing. This will likely involve additional investment in your infrastructure to automate the data flow into the model as well as automating the triggers for model re-calibration in case accuracy metrics are falling below acceptable limits.

9.11 Iterate!

Once you are done building and productionizing your model, you will get new insights from the model predictions. These predictions and insights can be used to refine your use case and problem statement. As you adjust your problem statement, you will repeat the above steps to continue updating and enhancing your model.

9.11 Summary Data Science Workflow

So in summary, you can visualize your data science workflow as follows:

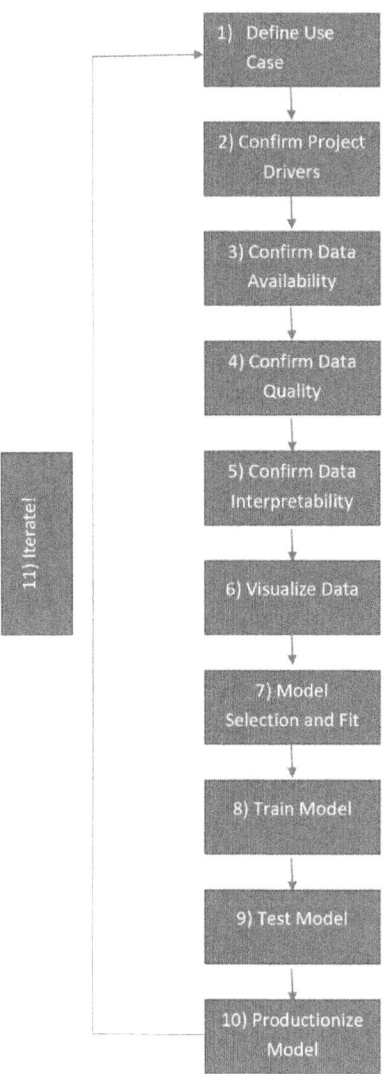

10. Conclusion

In summary, we started this book with an introduction to Python and covered the basics including the different data types and data structures. We then progressed to analyzing a real data set using foundational Python libraries like Pandas and Numpy. We learned to visualize and explore our data and determined how to exclude missing and outlier values.

We were also able to train and test two predictive models using different algorithms namely Linear Regression and Decision Tree Regression. We then learned about additional machine learning models as well as deep learning and neural networks.

Last but not least, we also covered how you can problem solve using machine learning algorithms and how to go from use case all the way to fully fleshed machine learning model.

We did all the above using visual examples and illustrations – using the power of Python!

I hope this book helped with your understanding of building machine learning models in Python and you feel more confident in getting hands-on with Python! Look for future books in this series to continue your data science journey!

Post your Review

Your review will help me improve this book and future content and will also help other readers find this book!

Thanks again for purchasing this book and your continued support!

Website and Free Gift!

Don't be a stranger and please check out my website:

https://www.daneyalauthor.com

You will be able to download all the Python code used in this book by visiting the above link.

References

1. Python Main Site: https://www.python.org/
2. Zen of Python: https://www.python.org/dev/peps/pep-0020/
3. Getting Started with Python: https://www.python.org/about/gettingstarted/
4. Anaconda Distribution: https://www.anaconda.com/distribution/
5. Jupyter Notebook: https://jupyter.org/
6. Galton, F. (1877). Regression in Statistical Analysis - Typical laws of heredity. III. Nature, 15(389), 512-514.

Printed in Great Britain
by Amazon

81140470R00041